Awake *and* Alive

Revolutionize Your Relationships through
Personal Revolution Therapy ™

● ● ● ● ● ● ●

DR. JAMES TRIANA

iUniverse, Inc.
Bloomington

Contents

Forward

Compassion, truth, and forbearance are the three basic elements that gave birth to Personal Revolution Therapy ™ (PRT).
-Dr. Triana-

As with many curious boys and girls who are hungry for adventure to explore the world around them, I too at an early age was curious. I sought to learn and explore the inner workings of the mind.

Attending elementary Catholic school was the perfect environment for me to start inquiring about the importance spirituality has in our lives. The earliest memory I recall is the time when I first asked questions about Catholicism in the second grade at my Catholic school in Jacksonville, Florida. For most Catholics, second grade is the year where seven-year-old children receive their First Communion. My classmates and I were no exception. I remember the nuns barely explaining why first communion is an important Catholic Sacrament. The nuns would only respond, "Because Jesus loves you." I remember walking away puzzled, thinking, "but Jesus loves everybody, Catholics or not."

A couple of days before making my First Communion, I approached a priest for the explanation to my unanswered question. I asked, "Father, why as Catholics do we need to pray to saints to communicate with God? Can't I communicate with God directly?" The priest looked at me, as if I had rudely interrupted his day and said, "Enough, get back to your classroom." I returned to my classroom more worried that I had bothered the priest than upset that my question was not answered. Determined to gain understanding, the next day I asked a different priest the same question. I asked, "Father, how come we have to fear God to be good Catholics?" Once again, the second priest also provided no satisfying answer to my question about what it means to be Catholic. His response to me was, " get to your classroom." Needless to say, I was left hanging with my questions unanswered while receiving my First Communion. I remember as a seven-year-old feeling spiritually disconnected to something that was obviously important to the Catholic Church.

My own metaphorical "wandering in the desert for forty years" lasted 25 years. As an adolescent, my parents allowed me to visit churches from different Christian denominations and synagogues in my quest to understand the importance of spirituality. It was not until I completed my Masters degree and started working as a counselor at a family-counseling center that I was introduced to the fundamentals of Eastern philosophy. One of my coworkers had a prolific understanding of Eastern philosophy. For the most part, this particular counseling center was enriched with 30 well experienced therapists who adopted Western traditional therapies of their liking to help their clients. However, many of these therapists did not incorporate any spirituality focus into their treatment plans with their clients. In our weekly client progress meetings, I began to notice the therapists who did not provide their clients the option to use spirituality as a tool for inner healing. I paid close attention to those therapists whose focus was only on Western traditional therapies. I began to see a pattern in the therapy reports from these treatment plans. In almost every case the therapists would report that their clients struggled to maintain the progress they have made. It was then that I started to search for ways to unite both Eastern and Western philosophies into effective treatment plans for my own clients.

Many therapists both then and now feel threatened to incorporate Western traditional therapies with Eastern philosophies to help their clients. However, my own spiritual journey has allowed me to discover that these two forces of healing can be a less threatening way for therapists to use with their clients. My research of progress reports has helped me to embrace both Eastern and Western religions that include Catholicism as well as Buddhism. The combination of these two philosophies can be the basis in which to provide practical techniques for clients to use on their own. I believe spirituality is an essential component to having a happy fulfilled life as well as an effective treatment plan.

My "aha" moment came to me in understanding that effective spiritual practice can be quantified and that spirituality is essential in the lives of many. Quantifying spirituality is possible by measuring physiological responses associated when one meditates or prays. Meditation or praying is different from relaxation techniques. I discovered that clients gained better insight about themselves through meditation or praying than from relaxation techniques. The former allows clients to be better universally connected to a radiant force that brings a sense of comfort to their own existence. This is what I call spiritual mental process work. Clients who just used relaxation techniques struggled because many still felt emotionally disconnected to forces beyond their control.

The problem with psychotherapy today is that most therapists deal with faith or spirituality passively in therapy sessions. Good therapists are trained to respect the religious beliefs of their patients but that is where it stops. Most therapists do not engage their patients to enrich their spirituality through mental process work.

Spirituality becomes dormant because most therapists lack the training in incorporating spirituality with traditional therapies. Clients hesitate to bring spirituality to sessions if the therapist takes a passive role or redirects the clients to non-spiritual problem solving. As a therapist I allow clients to speak about their religious beliefs. Then, when clients recognize an unbiased approach from me, clients become more motivated in their recovery. I notice this approach also prevents clients from terminating therapy prematurely once the psychological symptoms go away. I find this approach encourages clients to stay in therapy and seek possible deeper causes for their symptoms. This process uncovers new and healthier meanings for how the client chooses to direct their own life. Clients are able to get a clear perspective on their lives and gain better insight into their own behavior through traditional psychological treatments as well as doing their spiritual mental process work.

Over many years working in this way with clients I have witnessed clients gaining a deeper understanding of what the meaning of life is for them. Because they have a better understanding of their psychological and spiritual needs, they feel complete as a person and competent to tackle the diversities that life brings to them. The tools created in Personal Revolution Therapy are to be used whether or not you are in therapy. Therapy is not "happily ever after." Being psychologically and spiritually available to enjoy events in your life as they are happening NOW makes for sustaining a higher quality of life. Post-therapy without Eastern philosophy puts the client at risk to return to old bad habits. People and personal needs do change in any long-term relationship such as is in a spousal, parent/child, or coworker relationship. Therefore, creating a user-friendly treatment plan in which clients can learn and grow with has been my focus in the development of Personal Revolution Therapy.

Incorporating both Eastern and Western approaches to healing is essential for maintaining a fulfilled life. As a therapist, I don't have the answers for clients. However, what I tell them is, "lets work together as I present you with the mental tools to help you get to the path toward compassion and self understanding using Personal Revolution Therapy (PRT)." The next step, provide the client with PRT tools and TRUST that the client will do their own mental process work. I have not met a client who has put in the mental work and not found solutions to their own personal, psychological and spiritual issues. My message to others therapists is, "Revolutionize your therapy techniques by incorporating Eastern and Western healing practices." Eastern philosophy is not passive since most Eastern philosophies require one to meditate and meditation is very interactive and does require mental process work.

Acknowledgments

The discrepancy between what counseling textbooks say that should take place and what actually happens in counseling has bothered me since my early years as a graduate intern student. I feel honored that many people have helped me resolve this dilemma. I want to acknowledge all of my patients who were brave enough to want to make changes in their lives to improve their relationships. I would also like to thank my many colleagues who have help me refine and shape my ideas that went into developing the concepts of Personal Revolution Therapy ™

To my grandfather, Santiago Triana Cortez, M.D., whose desire was to improve the techniques of general surgery through medical research that inspired me also to develop better techniques to help people improve their own mental well-being. To my father, Santiago Hernan Triana, M.D. who treated his patience with respect rather than treating them as if they were just bodies with problems. He went above and beyond by really understanding the people he was treating. Also, my father's insightful philosophical views of the human spirit helped me stay focused on the principles expressed in this book. To my loving mother, Mariana Triana and my sister, Maggie for their constant emotional support and unconditional love. To my sister-in-law Frances Negron, professor at Columbia University and author, whose words inspired me to set the writing style for this book. Lastly, I am much appreciative of Professor Marianne Mason from Georgia State University for her time and feedback on this book.

I would also wish to express my appreciation to my neurological research colleagues, Dr. Richard Singer and Dr. Barry Cutler, for allowing me to work with them in clinical trials for dementia and how to develop effective clinical interventions. I also want to acknowledge Dr. Leon Shore for sharing his incredible knowledge about nutrition that not only helped me lose weight but also gave me an understanding of how I can better guide patients who wish to lose weight by using the techniques in this book. I also want to acknowledge Dr. Gregory Albert, plastic surgeon, for his time and collaboration in designing a program that would help improve the mental wellness of elective cosmetic surgery patients through the use of the techniques in this book.

I am forever appreciative to Helen Haruben and Allison Noonan for their many hours reviewing my manuscript and their guidance that went into this book. I want to also acknowledge Erik Halber for his help in creating my website that set forth the outline for this book.

$\cdots$ PART I $\cdots$

Introduction

Humankind, throughout the ages, has experienced and is experiencing many revolutions—political, socioeconomic, and technological. Despite this, people all over the world continue to struggle with the most important part of human life, Relationships! This happens in romantic, parent/child, employer/employee or athlete/coach relationships.

Why do people stay in relationships that are not working for them? In fact, why do many people ignore the warning signs in a relationship? The answer is that a large number of people do not have the effective coping skills necessary to solve problems that arise within that relationship. Many people stay in unsatisfying relationships for a long time hoping that any good that still exists in that relationship will miraculously come out and save the relationship. Also, in unhappy relationships, many people fail to see how their own personal needs have changed within that relationship. Without effective coping skills and/or self-awareness, many struggle to make adjustments to those changing needs.

Personal Revolution Therapy ™ (PRT) with its techniques can help give you key insights and strategies to improve your relationships. These PRT techniques: Sitting/Listening, Rethinking/Re-examining, Creating/Prioritizing Alternatives, and Executing your Plan are strategically designed to enhance inner awareness, improve thinking, set realistic goals, and follow through with action. I am introducing four mental tools that revolutionize how you relate to others. PRT skills teach you inner peace as well as help you make the changes needed to improve your relationships. PRT skills can be used whether you are in therapy of not. PRT techniques cannot only help you improve your own relationships, but the techniques can also be used to teach your children so that they can also develop healthy relationships as adolescents and adults.

The mastering of these unique PRT techniques results in getting your personal needs met on a daily basis. Achieving the skills needed to improve your relationships and maintain a path of making good decisions in your life does not come from just sitting and reading "how to" books or by merely understanding what you just read. It comes from you allowing yourself to take that first risk and see yourself as an individualized and loving person.

PRT techniques provide practical methods in how to avoid repeating the same mistakes. To err is human but repeating the same mistakes in relationships is problematic. Many times we miss seeing our own repeated mistakes in our relationships because ourselves do not always so easily see the driving forces behind them. PRT techniques offer the tools to correct repeated mistakes through exploration and understanding of those repeated mistakes.

Personal Revolution Therapy ™ techniques help you get a better understanding of yourself. For, "know thy self" is the greatest weapon in improving your relationship with others. Knowing thyself is what gives a person the persistence and desire to find solutions to any type of relationship problems.

Why we need Personal Revolution Therapy (PRT)

Just as in a political or socioeconomic revolution, **relationship revolution** also requires effective coping skills for maintaining or improving your relationship with others, whether you are in a healthy or unhealthy relationship. Developing interpersonal coping skills, and seeing its advantages in any relationship are intricate parts of a successful personal revolutionary journey. There is no greater personal reward than mastering inner awareness and implementing effective social skills with others to bring about enjoyable and satisfying relationships with your love ones and those whom you come in contact with. PRT tools are not only used in intimate relationships, but also to help you build up your confidence in communicating with others in unpleasant unexpected encounter with others such as bank tellers or strangers.

Personal Revolution Therapy strategies start by encouraging you to ask yourself several fundamental questions. What is it that you perceive is lacking in your present troubled relationship with another person? What is keeping you from finding inner peace? The initial problem about finding inner peace is that we genuinely want inner peace but often we are not sure of how to get it. In trying to solve a conflicted relationship, it is a common mistake to think that "someone else or something else" will bring inner peace into our lives. What frequently happens is that we fail in finding inner peace because we believe that the other person has in their possession your key to your inner peace. To think that that person or thing will bring you inner peace is misleading. The answer to the fundamental questions maybe simply that you lack the coping skills needed to tackle difficult relationships. Having problems in any relationship may feel like the other person in the relationship is preventing you from having inner peace. However, reality is that only you can give yourself the inner peace you seek. I created PRT strategies to show you how to really revolutionize your daily interactions with others, to give you the inner peace you seek.

Personal Revolution Therapy skills help you learn how to use strategic skills whether you are faced with one problem or multiple problems in your relationships. Difficult relationships cause us to struggle daily with stress in our lives. Managing multiple problems can feel unmanageable. Suddenly, we find ourselves taking on too much at once and before you know it, we are making mistakes that could have been avoided. This can produce chronic stress that weakens our ability to concentrate and to resolve conflict effectively. Our quality of life diminishes which often causes us to take time off from work or we may suffer from not being able to spend quality time with our families. With these PRT strategies not only are you able to solve relationship problems, but they also prevent you from repeating the same mistakes by prioritizing your needs associated with each problem, making your life more manageable.

PRT Techniques better prepares you to RESPOND rather than to REACT to any encounter that comes your way in relationships. When we respond to interactions with others we move TOWARD finding solutions to relationship problems. When we react to interactions with others we move AWAY from finding ways to resolve relationship problems. When you react to relationship problems, your judgment becomes unclear and you tend to react more impulsively without recognizing the consequences of your actions. Reacting before thinking usually gets you into trouble and feeling regretful. However, when we respond to relationship issues we are taking accountability for our actions. It empowers you to have the ability to think things through before doing anything. This thinking process allows you time to create and execute healthier alternatives in dealing with any problems. PRT techniques give you those mental tools and time for you to look over all possible options without having to sacrifice your own values and principles to get what you want. PRT techniques offer you the ability to think for yourself. PRT skills are self-empowering mental tools that you have when you are trying to resolve difficult relationship issues in your life.

What makes for happy or unhappy relationships

Why do we want relationships in the first place? Having healthy relationships with others provides us with three essential emotional needs. The first is having Inner peace, or self-harmony. The second reason is to bond with others and the third reason is the need to have a sense of belonging. As social beings, these three needs must be met to have a fulfilling and meaningful life.

There are two basic facts as to what makes for unhappy relationships. First, not clearly knowing what your own needs are in any given relationship. Second, not knowing how to get those needs met. Being in a difficult relationship can prevent us from having inner peace. Without inner peace, we struggle to make good decisions, even during times of political and economical stability. When our inner world feels unsettled, many times we do not recognize our own mistakes until it is too late. We then must deal with the consequences of our actions. This can be exhausting to the body as well as the mind. We find ourselves easily fatigued like coming back from an emotional war zone that sometimes causes health problems to develop.

When the body begins to break down so does the mind and spirit.

The pitfall of a broken mind and spirit in any troubled

relationship is that we are not aware that our needs are not being met. We do not communicate with the other person that our needs may be changing and also not being met. Our emotional and psychological needs are constantly changing in any mature and loving relationship. As long as we know that this is happening and we keep the communication open and truthful, this is good for the relationship. Unfortunately, this rarely occurs in most relationships no matter what type of relationship you are in. This happens in romantic, parent/child or employer/employee relationships.

Coping with these emotional and psychological changes do not come automatically to us. We are not born with the capabilities to apply these coping skills immediately. These skills must be learned. What do come naturally are those bad feelings that accompany us in any unsatisfying relationship. When problems arise within any relationship, we must have in our possession, at all times, access to our own coping skills to avoid further breakdown in that relationship. PRT skills give us the ability to help us be more aware and ready to make flexible adjustments to solve whatever problem is arising with you and the other person.

Being aware of your own needs is an important part of being in a happy relationship. You must abolish false expectations about what you would want out of that relationship and replace it with realistic expectations that reflect your needs. Knowing what you truly need from the other person makes for having a fulfilling loving relationship. In order to have a clear idea about your current needs, PRT techniques can be used to identify those needs.

Personal Revolution Therapy ™ (PRT)

HOW WAS **PRT** DEVELOPED?

Personal Revolution Therapy ™ (PRT) was developed from my 30 years of providing therapy to individuals and families. In my efforts to further help my clients, not only learn, but also apply new coping skills, I developed PRT strategies. You will notice that throughout this book there are bolded words. These bolded words I feel are important for you to familiarize yourself with. These words will help you better understand some basic dynamics of relationship interaction. This will give you insight when you begin using the PRT techniques yourself.

Another part that went into designing PRT strategies was incorporating Western approaches to healing with techniques from Eastern philosophies. Much of my clinical experience came from years of training in using solid Western traditional therapies as a therapeutic intervention to help others who suffered from emotional and psychological problems. I discovered that when I included Eastern approaches to healing, a more holistic way to look at relationships, AND applied Western traditional therapy techniques, clients took more of an initiative to remove their own negative emotional "reflectors." This also allows them to be more receptive to problem solving. Blending Western and Eastern approaches to healing is a new way of thinking of how you are going to solve your relationship problems. I saw that when clients used these PRT techniques, they really revolutionized their thinking processes which empowered them to act more effectively to any present or potential problem that could arise when relating to others.

What does Western traditional therapies and Eastern philosophies have to do with you wanting to improve relationships with others? By combining both approaches you not only learn coping skills to work through troubled relationships, but they also help you reevaluate your personal meaning of life. I refer to Western traditional therapies to be techniques that have proven through research in helping people deal with psychological problems. Most traditional therapies focuses on how emotional symptoms stemming from a difficult relationship are affecting the individual. Adding Eastern approaches to the healing process enables you to explore yourself more holistically. That is, Eastern approaches to healing wants to help you look, not only at your problem, but also look at your existing emotional strengths for solving that problem. I noticed that when I combined both approaches in PRT strategies, many of my clients were able to tackle problems more effectively.

WESTERN APPROACHES TO HEALING

Western approaches to healing have been effective in reducing psychological symptoms for generations. Using traditional therapies can treat symptoms like depression, anxiety and addiction. Some traditional forms of therapy are Behavior Therapy, Cognitive Therapy, or Psychodynamic Therapy. Behavior therapists believe that it is our behavior that is the root of our psychological symptoms. Behavior therapists focus on adjusting or changing a person's environment so that a person is less tempted to repeat bad behaviors from the previous unhealthy environment. This behavior therapy is used most commonly with people who suffer from addiction. That is why sometimes therapists suggest that people who seek treatment for addiction find a detox program away from where the addicted person lives.

Cognitive therapists believe it is how we think that creates suffering in our lives. Cognitive therapists focus on learning how to think more effectively to improve relationships. Brainstorming to seek solutions to personal problems is a common technique used by cognitive therapists to help people improve their lives.

Psychodynamic therapists believe that it is how we interact with each other that determine if we develop psychological symptoms. Psychodynamic therapists focus on helping people resolve any feelings of inferiority, inadequacies, and insecurities that exist in their lives. Psychodynamic therapy helps people achieve a sense of personal power and positive social feelings.

I see now in my clients that traditional therapies ARE an important part of good therapy, but too frequently something happens afterwards. Many clients drop out of therapy too early before gaining enough self-awareness and self-confidence to use good mental tools. As a result their symptoms can easily recur. I questioned, as many other clinical practitioners, why this happens? One theory I consider is that traditional therapies focus mainly on treating psychological symptoms and not the cause. I found out that many clients discontinued traditional therapy after the symptoms were eliminated. What became common and interesting for me to see in my sessions was that the same clients returned to therapy because their symptoms had resurfaced. Clients would again drop out of therapy when their symptoms were gone.

Western approaches to healing became a revolving door of

fragmented sessions, offering no opportunity for clients to work through those relationships that the client felt were the cause of their symptoms in the first place. It became important for me to show people not only how to reduce psychological symptoms, but to also provide them long lasting mental tools, like PRT skills, to work through any difficult relationship. As a result of observing many clients with similar difficulties in their treatment, I developed PRT strategies which includes Eastern approaches to healing.

EASTERN APPROACHES TO HEALING

PRT incorporates Eastern approaches to healing, as an approach to help you use a bigger "canvas," or having more emotional awareness, to create your world where all your needs are met. In discovering PRT techniques, I realized I not only needed to help clients relieve their depressive or anxious symptoms, but I also needed to assist them in painting a better picture of their needs to reflect their overall dreams.

Many Eastern approaches to healing provides us with the ingredients to have healthy relationships. The "canvas" of your mental awareness must be made from 1) seeking the truth about your needs, 2) showing your compassion without self-sacrifice and 3) having forbearance or self control. Having an Eastern approach to healing refers to a state of awareness. Awareness is the main ingredient needed in beginning your journey to making healthier relationships.

Let me briefly explain each mental state of awareness. First, in Eastern approaches to healing "seeking the truth about your needs," encourages you to understand fundamentally that your own needs can only be fulfilled or changed by you. Our needs are measured based on how good we feel or how positive our thinking is as well as by seeing favorable outcomes of our actions. What other people do or say to you can threaten your needs from being met. Many times it comes down to knowing that you and only you must establish first what your needs are now before jumping into doing anything about it.

The second state of awareness is, "showing your compassion without self sacrifice." This state of awareness strengthens the understanding that you can show compassion without sacrificing your needs. Many times we believe that to have compassion for others we must sacrifice our well being, including our personal identity. This is untrue. In tough relationships, having sympathy and desire to alleviate the suffering of loved ones does not mean for you to have to sacrifice your own needs. In my office, I noticed many clients struggle to answer the question, "Who are you?" Many say they are a wife, mother, daughter, sister or a friend. Next, I ask them to elaborate on what makes them who they are. Most say, "by doing things for the people in my life." I have found that many women cannot define who they are. They only have an identity if they are doing something for someone else. This often happens because they do not know their needs or value themselves enough. Being in a state of awareness can reveal to you its limitations of why are you not getting your needs met. It also helps you to realize your identity may be dependent of what you do for others. Therefore, you need to know that you can still show compassion to others without compromising your needs.

The third mental state of awareness is, "having forbearance or self control." In stressful times, in conflicted relationships you may do something that jeopardizes your well-being. As long as you think the other person has control over your behavior, you relinquish your power to the other person over your own behavior. Therefore, you may struggle in re-examining your needs freely. What the other person may say or do can INFLUENCE how you think and feel. ULTIMATELY you have the control to choose how to handle the outcome of how you think, feel or react to the problems of any relationship.

Eastern approaches to healing views interdependent relationships as the ideal framework for having and maintaining good relationships. Interdependent relationships focus on the balance between the giving of yourself without sacrificing your needs and also allowing yourself to receive kindness from others. Having interdependent relationships allows for the reflection of inner acceptance, not of what you have done to get recognition from another person. Eastern approaches to healing consider "Unhealthy" to mean too clingy, too dependent, too distant, or totally independent within a relationship. When this happens, your needs are not being met in that relationship. A harmony of "give" and "take" is what makes for a healthy relationship. PRT techniques are developed from Eastern philosophy to healing. Practicing and incorporating the three mental states of awareness based on Eastern philosophy helps you gain a **clear mindset** as you start using PRT techniques.

Things To Watch Out For Before Starting To Use PRT Techniques

After treating hundreds of clients, I have noticed similar patterns that cause my clients to struggle to make changes in their lives. One pattern that often occurs is that clients can cultivate an understanding of their problems, but have difficulty implementing an effective plan based on their knowledge alone. When clients read self-help books, I notice clients understand the reasons for their problems, or problems of their love ones, yet they continue to have difficulty putting that knowledge into practice. I recall Betty who is the mother of a child diagnosed with Attention Defiant Disorder. Betty had come to my office carrying books and journals about this condition. She was well informed and updated about the condition. Even though Betty had exposure to data, statistics and a wealth of "how-to" advice about handling ADD she continued to struggle. Betty was unable to effectively translate what she was reading about the disorder into skills that could potentially help her son. What was the problem?

Betty was so invested in her son's condition that she was **unaware** of her own struggles to help him. Not being aware of how you are being affected when seeing loved ones suffer is a pattern I notice in most of my clients regardless of the problems they bring to therapy. This is called **Mental Barriers.** Often watching our own family member suffer can be so very painful that we do not pay attention to our own suffering. Being unaware of our own suffering can be a survival mechanism when we try to keep the family intact in time of crisis. **Mental Barriers** are created when we are unaware and unskilled to process what is going on inside us. I notice many clients are unaware of their **Mental Barriers** because they feel exhausted and helpless in solving their relationship problems. However, even though clients feel moments of hopelessness, they all seem to share a common thread; a tremendous desire to help themselves and their loved ones.

Throughout my years of clinical practice, I have observed in my clients some common barriers that have prevented them from reaching personalized inner peace in their relationships. Some barriers work in subtle ways that we sometimes do not even see or recognize being present. We find ourselves compromising our needs and doing things that pull us away from the real problems of that relationship. We start saying things like, "I can't live without him," or "I will never love again." "If I change, he will change," or "if we have another child our marriage will get better." What exactly are the mental barriers? I have discovered 3 common barriers that prevent us from clearing the way and having wonderful relationships. The first barrier is **denial.**

Denial is evident when a person is unaware there is a problem and continues to repeat the same mistakes within that relationship. For example, a person who constantly sacrifices their own well-being and becomes unknowingly mentally enslaved to the needs of the other person. Throughout my years in practice, I listened to many women share about the years of dedication they gave to their spouse, children and extended relatives. These women were unaware they had lost their own identity years ago. Denial and lack of awareness left them feeling dissatisfied in most of their relationships. Their identities had been connected for so long to what they did for others and not of whom they are as a people. Being in this state of denial, produces a recurrence of starting other unhealthy relationships. How many times have you told yourself that you will never date anyone like that again? Then, when the new relationship begins to have the same problems as the previous relationship, regret sets in, you tell yourself, "See, I did it again." This brings me to the second barrier, **avoidance.**

Avoidance is evident when you are in a conflicted relationship and both persons ignore the problem by not addressing it. This is usually accompanied by one or both persons feeling fearful that if the problem is to be confronted then the problem could get worst. The longer you let time pass by not dealing with the problem, the more controversial feelings about the relationship will intensify. Usually, consciously or unconsciously, we start displaying self destructive behaviors in hopes those bad feelings will go away. Self-destructive behaviors like abusing alcohol or having an affair are examples and indicators that we are in avoidance.

The third barrier is **displacing. Displacing** is evident when we take our frustrations out on other people. We do this to try and rid ourselves of overwhelming feelings of distress, which usually accompanies unsolved problematic relationships. This happens in most people who do not have the right coping skills to resolve problems in their conflicted relationships. Sadly enough, most of the individuals who are targets of emotional displacement are people whom we love. For example, the fearful employee who can not talk to his or her boss about a work related problem and goes home and yells at a family member for no reason. Many times in my office I work with couples that initially come in for therapy because they are concerned for their child who is having behavioral problems. In some cases, **displacing** was evident when the parents pay attention ONLY to their child's problem without taking into consideration how their marital problems may be affecting their child's behavior. In my clinical practice I have observed many children who see their parents fight often will purposely or unconsciously act out. Many kids believe that by acting out will deter their parents from more fighting, therefore keeping the family together.

Unacknowledged barriers destroy families as well as prevent us from identifying which barriers exist and to what degree they adversely affect our lives. The good news is, once we understand how much these 3 barriers play a role in preventing us from improving and creating healthy relationships, we are better prepared to apply PRT techniques.

PRT techniques are purposely designed to solve a variety of relationship problems, whether you are in therapy or not. PRT techniques are effective and simple with clear steps that you can also teach your children. In my clinical practice as I listened to children, adolescents, and adult clients speak of wanting to learn practical ways to solve relationship problems, I realized I needed to offer a "mental tool box" that clients could use at anytime. As a result, I developed PRT techniques so that clients of all ages and from all educational backgrounds can adapt to their own situations. The only prerequisite needed for a person to improve their relationships with others is a desire for change. By tackling relationship troubles at the moment a problem arises will prevent any mental barrier from developing.

Fortunately for most of the human population, we have an inner ability to know when something is wrong, but we lack the physical and emotional awareness to recognize such issues. Recognizing there is a "disturbance in the force" or being aware of the cues our bodies send us is the key to successfully changing how we respond to difficult relationships. This is the most important ingredient to have in order to successfully use PRT tools.

Taking personal accountability to confront any relationship

problem can create wondrous possibilities for you to learn and use PRT techniques throughout your lifetime. Most of us are born with abilities to change ourselves, our lives and our relationships for the better. And instead of having false expectations that others will change for you, PRT skills will help you work on yourself first so you can bring genuine success into your relationships.

•• PART II ••

PRT Techniques

In this section, I will describe four innovative techniques that will help improve or create satisfying relationships. First, I will define each strategy. Second, I will discuss how I applied these strategies with my patients. And finally, I will show you how you can apply these strategies on your own.

First Technique - Sitting and Listening

The first technique, "Sitting and Listening" incorporates both Eastern forms of meditation as well as the practice of prayer in Western cultures.

In our busy lives as we are constantly attempting to balance our relationships with others, we sometimes find ourselves too busy to sit and listen to our own thoughts. Sadly, we often prefer to pay more attention to strangers or characters in the media than to ourselves. When we do not take the opportunity to focus on ourselves, what sets forth is the potential for establishing poor interactions with others. What happens?

During any relationship dispute in which we start experiencing negative attitudes towards another person, we start doing destructive behaviors toward the person who upset us. If you do not work through these negative attitudes and destructive behavior patterns of abuse, this will start to accumulate into a "snowball" effect. We get jumpy. We may say things that we really don't mean. By Sitting and Listening, that is, you simply stop what you are doing, sit, catch your breath and listen to your breathing. Now listen patiently to your rapid thoughts. This will stop the "snowball" effect before more damage can occur to the relationship. By "Sitting and Listening" you start focusing more on how your own thoughts and feelings are affecting your relationship with that other person. We let others think they are in control of our own thoughts and feelings when we angrily focus on what that other person might be doing to us.

A parent once told me that she was going to therapy because of her daughter's misconduct. I responded to her by saying, "you mean you are going to therapy because of the feelings YOU have toward your daughter." Negative thinking about another person, like this mother toward her daughter, can worsen or prevent you from making any real efforts to improve that relationship. Intense negative thinking about any relationship can cause more stress. Stress can "blind" us from exploring any constructive ways to improve that relationship. Therefore, stop the stress by first starting to just sit for a moment. Then, you listen openly to your thoughts and feel the environment around you. It is not what others do to you, but what you think they are doing to you.

Since we rely on our emotions and past experiences to define the quality of our relationships, negative thinking can mislead us in seeing clearly both the good and bad of relationships. I notice many of my clients have the tendency to jump to conclusions and act impulsively without having the skills to stop negative thinking. "Sitting and Listening" helps you to catch your breath and think first before acting. The purpose of "Sitting and Listening" is to help you slow down your thinking. As parents, how many times do we find ourselves saying to our children, "you should have stopped and thought about that first."

"Sitting and Listening" can be effective even in serious relationship problems like domestic violence. Many family members struggle to let their "guard" down. Lowering your "guard" so you can "Sit and Listen" may not be a luxury for families of domestic violence. The risk can be very harmful. However, when imminent physical danger is not present, I have seen some family members take the challenge to "Sit and Listen." By doing so, sometimes they come to realizations about things such as how they view the understanding of the word anger.

"Sitting and Listening" allows family members to feel less frightened and more empowered to courageously do something about the problem. A small "door" of understanding begins to emerge in their minds about their own barriers. For example, the barrier that anger as anger has power and should never be expressed inappropriately OR appropriately, can stop people from making necessary changes in their lives. In my office, I will ask for the person to say aloud, "I feel angry." When that person sees no one is getting hurt when that is said, there is a sensation of freedom that they feel as if they are "removing a mental gag from their mouths" by expressing their anger out loud.

How can I use PRT's "Sitting and Listening" techniques on my own to help me improve my relationships with others? What do I do to improve any conflict with any person that I care about? Remember that the goal of "Sitting and Listening" is to slow down your negative thinking in order to regroup, making room for learning better thinking patterns which is PRT's next technique. This reduces your emotional and physical stress.

You first start by paying attention to your breathing. This helps you regain your thought before doing something that you might regret later. PRT's breathing techniques are so simple that you and your five-year-old child can easily learn them, even if you are not in therapy. As I have coached clients to do breathing exercises in my office, you can do the same for yourself at home. Start by inhaling through your nose, slowly allowing your chest to expand. Then, breath out through your mouth slowly as you are feeling your chest cave in. Do this three times. Slow breathing will also slow down your thoughts and allow you to think more clearly before reacting negatively to a situation. Consistent practice of this breathing exercise will improve your health and wellbeing as well as improve your communication in all your relationships.

When can you use this technique? Should I use this technique in all circumstances? PRT's "Sitting and Listening" is about clearing out any barriers of stress and negative thinking. Do not worry about what is next. For right now all you need to do is just listen to your breathing and your heart rate. You will notice your breathing and your heart rate slow down. By "Sitting and Listening" you will be able to stop the "vicious cycle" of feeling stressed and hopeless about that unhealthy relationship. How we view our relationships and the feelings associated to that relationship is PRT's second technique, rethinking and re-examining.

SECOND TECHNIQUE- RETHINKING AND RE-EXAMINING

The second technique, "Rethinking and Re-examining your Thoughts" is about shifting your negative thinking to productive thinking. "Rethinking and Re-examining" is also about identifying your needs. We learn in "Sitting and Listening" how to slow down negative thinking. At this stage, we begin by asking a series of questions to help us identify what is it that we really want out of that troubled relationship. Try not to be judgmental but rather ask each question that will lead to an answer of optimism to avoid negative thinking. Here, "Rethinking and Re-examining your thoughts" is about firmly stating your needs. It is about clarifying exactly what you are wanting out of that relationship. As an airplane pilot would check the plane to see that all technical systems are working properly before taking off, "Rethinking and Re-examining Your Thoughts" is basically checking and clearing all your mental systems before taking action. Many times we "fly off the handle" too soon. We create more problems by not taking the time to think out the problem thoroughly. For example, when we say things like, "I want to spend more quality time together" or "I will no longer allow myself to be abused by you" or "these are my values and principles and they are non negotiable," we are sending reactionary statements to that other person. Taking the time to rethink these reactionary statements before they are said will improve how your words will be received.

What is the advantage of using the "Rethinking and Re-examining" technique? By asking a series of clear and concise questions about your true needs, it will help you reduce stress and shift from negative thinking to constructive thinking. This is what I call strategic orientation to your "Rethinking and Re-examining" process. Under stress we tend to act more impulsively without having a clear picture of the consequences. As you are listening to your thoughts ask, "What fears am I having about this relationship? How is this relationship impacting my life right now?" These techniques will help calm your thoughts and reduce any tension in your body that you may be experiencing.

Poor decision-making comes from not paying attention to your own thoughts. We get stuck focusing on the other person and expecting the other person to take the first step and change. What usually happens is that we get disappointed. "Rethinking and Re-examining" is about YOUR thoughts and your thoughts only. Listening to another person's thoughts and needs comes later. How am I supposed to understand what you need if I, myself, do not know what exactly I need for myself? "Rethinking and Re-examining" is not about focusing on the other person's thoughts or feelings. This is how false expectations are created which is then followed by regret. Regret is a good indicator that we have "jumped the gun." How many times have we said to ourselves, "You better change or I will leave you." Or when you ask yourself, "Did I need to scream at my son that way?" Or, "Did I need to sleep with him?" Ignoring your own thoughts and not knowing what you want out of that relationship builds negative thinking and false expectations. Once you have allowed yourself and your thoughts to slow down, you will begin to understand your own needs. Once you have gained that understanding you will be ready for the next step, PRT technique #3, "Creating and Prioritizing Alternatives." It is here where you will begin to change your thinking by consciously choosing a new path to productive communication.

THIRD TECHNIQUE- CREATING AND PRIORITIZING ALTERNATIVES

Now that your thoughts are calm and you know what you want, you can enter PRT's third technique, "Creating and Prioritizing Alternatives." In this step you will write down a few different alternatives to how you are going to solve that relationship problem. After your thoughts have been calmed by using PRT's "Sitting and Listening" and after you have shifted negative thinking to constructive thinking in "Rethinking and Re-examining," you are ready to address the problematic relationship with confidence and determination. You will know when you are ready because you will have discovered what your needs are from that relationship. You are now ready to put the first alternative into action.

Why do we need to have more than one Alternative? First, it

will reduce your stress because you will not be putting all your eggs in one basket. Second, if the first alternative fails, you can try the next one on the list. Also, sometimes the other person may not be ready to be receptive to any of your alternatives. The other person may have their own unresolved issues, which typically have nothing to do with you. What if none of my alternatives are well received? What do I do next? You rewrite your alternative list. This time, emphasize your values and principles and compare them to that relationship. Having alternatives is the antibiotic to fear and unrealistic expectations.

This PRT technique prepares you to have more confidence in yourself and less self-doubt about you taking action. It also prevents outsiders from interfering or influencing your choices. Having no alternatives forces us to have an urgency to do something sooner without exploring more productive alternatives to a problem. Our bias about the problems leads us to believe that if something is not done immediately "the whole world will tumble down." This state of mind gives rise to fear and resistance. Implementing PRT Alternatives technique reduces that fear and resistance.

It is important to remember that if you have never done anything different before in your troubled relationships until now that you will need to practice. Taking steps towards positive change takes work but I assure you that if you follow these steps you will be successful. You will see positive result and begin to feel your universal flow more regularly. Once you have established a plan for yourself based on a few options, you are ready to begin PRT technique #4 "Executing Your Plan".

Fourth Technique -Executing your Plan

The fourth technique is "Executing your Plan", or putting your plan into action. Lets first recap what you have learned in the previous three PRT techniques. Your nerves are now calmed from the stress created by the conflicted relationship. You started paying more attention to your inner world as you listened to your relaxed breathing. By doing so, you noticed your rapid thoughts had slowed down, allowing you to think more clearly. Then, in the second PRT technique, through your calmer thoughts, you were able to rethink and prioritize what is it that you really want out of that problematic relationship without having to sacrifice your own sense of worth. In the third PRT technique, you compiled a list of options to select from as you begin "Executing your Plan" to resolve your relationship problem with that other person.

In the fourth technique, "Executing your Plan", you focus on the idea that "I am responsible for my own feelings, thoughts, and actions and not responsible for the feelings, thoughts or actions of the other person." You keep in mind that you hold in your mental toolbox a selection of options to choose from for solving any specific problem in that relationship. You now execute your first prioritized option. If the other person does not like your first option for whatever reason, you move on to option two. This is not to say that your first option was a poor option. It just means that the other person was not receptive to that particular option. PRT skills remind you that you do not have control over the feelings, thoughts or behavior of the other person.

That is why you must be prepared to have alternatives when handling any relationship problems. We all make the mistake of thinking that we "are pretty sure" of how the other person is going to react. We may say things like "Obviously, I have known my husband for so many years. Don't you think I know him by now?" It is always better to have options in going about solving relationship problems. The truth is that our personal needs are constantly changing throughout the years, no matter how long we have been in that relationship. That is why we "Execute the Plan" always from a list of options because we can never be certain that the other person will respond the same way as before. That person's needs may have changed as well as your own needs. And remember, you can go back through any and all of the PRT techniques at any time, especially if you find yourself escalating and resorting to old behavior patterns. It is normal to struggle as we change so please do not expect yourself to be perfect as you are learning this new communication skill. It is very important to be patient with yourself.

$\cdot\cdot$ PART III $\cdot\cdot$

PRT Techniques In Action

Be Patient as you learn how to use PRT techniques

Learning how to use Personal Revolution Therapy techniques is a learning process. Be patient with yourself as you learn how to use PRT Techniques. Learning to use PRT techniques is the same as learning anything for the first time. It feels unnatural in the beginning but as you start using these PRT skills, however, you will become more comfortable in using them. The emotional experience that usually occurs when you start using PRT techniques is like the experience you had as a kid when you were learning how to ride a bicycle for the first time. It took some time to acquire the skills in learning how to ride a bike.

Do you remember how scary it felt the first time you got on that bicycle? And despite your fears of falling you were still able to maintain a level of excitement as you were learning how to ride? You might recall your parent instructing you to pay attention to all the coordination skills needed to succeed in being able to ride your bike. Your parent might have said to you something like, "keep both hands on the handlebar. Look straight ahead...keep your eyes on the road...focus on your balance." As you first sat on your bicycle, you were nervous and lacked self-confidence. The same thing will occur for you during the learning phase of the PRT techniques.

After several times of falling off your bike and getting back on it, something mentally started happening. After your skills improved in riding your bicycle, you noticed that you did not need to pay as much attention to the coordination skills needed to ride a bike. You became more confident and felt more natural in riding your bike after that. Why did that happen? Your learned knowledge of how to ride a bike was now stored in your long-term memory as a mental toolbox for you to use next time you went riding on your bike. In general, any learned skills, like painting or sporting, are stored in your brain unconsciously AFTER you have learned that skill. Starting to learn how to use PRT techniques follows the same learning process.

Learning to use PRT techniques at first may feel unnatural but the more you get back on your "bike" and continue to use these skills, the easier it will become to know how to use PRT skills to improve your relationships. This will lead you to feel more confident to know that PRT techniques are becoming a specific mental toolbox for you to use in helping you improve your relationships with others. Knowing how to use PRT techniques just becomes another learned skill for you to use daily in all your interpersonal relationships.

Once you have acquired these PRT techniques they will become apart of your personalized mental toolbox for use in improving your relationships with others. As you make PRT techniques your own, you will have more desire and be more persistent at "Executing Your Plan."

Of course, if the other person with whom you are having the relationship problem with is less cooperative in working with you to solve those problems in the relationship, improving that relationship becomes more challenging. Sadly enough, there is a high percentage of people who are in conflicted relationship that might resist working out those problems with you. Those individuals usually have a harder time breaking away from using their Mental Barriers. Because of what I see in my clinical practice in helping people solve different problems, I specifically developed PRT Techniques for you to use whether or not the other person is willing to work with you or not. Using PRT techniques regularly helps you be more persistent and motivated at finally getting what you want because now your mental forces are driven by your personal values and principles of how to have a healthy relationship.

Trust your instincts and allow yourself to work through each PRT technique thoroughly before moving on to the next PRT technique. It can take you an hour or a day to complete each PRT technique, especially the first technique, PRT Sitting and Listening. For some people, they might need to stay in the first PRT technique before moving on the next PRT technique for a week. It is not that those individuals are not utilizing the PRT technique properly. By you allowing yourself to "Sit and Listen" without you eagerly forcing yourself to move on to the next PRT technique, you allow your natural intuition to complete the job. That is, removing all unexpected mental triggers that could cause you to relapse. This is why I call PRT a personal revolutionary experience. It is YOU who decides what areas in your life you want to work on whether in relationships or self-achievements for personal growth. You OWN your PRT Techniques because it will help you genuinely achieve that inner peace.

PRT and Romantic Relationships

Harry and Sally came to my office for help because they were having relationship problems. They had met through online dating while each of them were still married to someone else. They continued that arrangement until they both moved in together months later after both got divorced. Both Harry and Sally admitted to not being honest with each other at the start of their relationship. They both even had been untruthful answering the questions on their own online dating profile. But because of their growing love that each one was feeling toward one another, they both did not want the relationship to end and wanted to work on improving their relationship.

For years Harry thrived as a successful medical doctor throughout his community. Yet for years in his private life he had been unsuccessful in achieving a healthy relationship with any women that he got romantically involved with. Harry came from divorced parents. Before his parents divorced, Harry would painfully witness his parents argue constantly about his father's infidelities and drinking problem. Harry remembers one time, while out with his friends, seeing his father engaging flirtatiously with strange woman. When Harry confronted his father about what he had seen, his father made him swear to secrecy not to tell his mother for, "it would devastate her already weak nerves." Harry, himself, grew up being a womanizer like his father and used his doctoral title and money as means to lure women to have sex with him. After he seduced a woman, he would get tired of her, end that relationship and start on his next womanizing quest.

Sally was a very beautiful and vigorous woman who used those attributes to attract men into her life. Sally was a victim of childhood sexual abuse by her uncle. A sexual abuse history that lasted for most of her preadolescent and adolescent years by her uncle and who constantly threatened to harm her if she would tell anybody about the abuse. In her later adolescent years, Sally finally got the courage to tell her mother about the abuse. Unfortunately, her mother did not believe her about the abuse and got violent with her. Her mother beat her so severely that it left Sally with multiple cuts and bruises throughout her face and body. Her mother made Sally swear to not tell "such lies." As one would expect, Sally grew up having difficulties trusting people, especially, in romantic relationships with men. For Sally, it was not so much about having a romantic relationship with a man as it was in controlling that relationship with sex for self-preservation.

Harry and Sally started having relationship problems shortly after they both moved in together. Sally traveled a lot because of her work and Harry started feeling suspicious that Sally was cheating on him. Even though Sally had not said or done anything that would make Harry suspicious that she was cheating, he still felt he could not trust her. Sally became more irritated with Harry each time he would accuse her of cheating and their arguments became more intense. They started to have incidents of verbal and physical altercations with one another.

When I introduced Harry and Sally to the Personal Revolution Therapy techniques, I first encouraged each of them to stop being verbally and physically abusive toward each other and to be faithful to one another. Since PRT techniques are about self-discovery, I started working individually with first Harry then Sally in helping each one of them to develop their own PRT techniques. This approach helped both Harry and Sally later when they used their own PRT techniques to work directly on their relationship problems.

During the next several months as I introduced and explained PRT techniques to Harry, he was gradually able to improve his relationship with Sally through repeatedly practicing the techniques of PRT.

Harry struggled at first in using the "Sitting and Listening" technique. Harry's arrogance viewed the idea of "Sitting and Listening" in paying attention to his own breathing as something that was beneath him to do. "For Pete's sake, I'm the one telling my patience at my office to relax," he said. Harry was accustomed in wanting to "fix" things or in this case, Sally. He would ask me, "Can you just tell me how to stop being jealous and help me convince Sally that I am not a bad guy?" Obviously, Harry was not ready to use the "Sitting and Listening" technique yet. He would later discover that listening to his own breathing brought back bad childhood memories, an insight that helped him return to and use the "Sitting and Listening" technique.

Harry, however, was able to apply and gain better insight about himself in using PRT's "Rethinking and Re-examining" technique, which helped him focus more on himself than on Sally. I started by asking Harry a series of non-threatening questions about any memories of happy childhood experiences and gradually asking about unhappy childhood memories. Harry quickly began talking about his athleticism as a kid and of his many football touchdowns and baseball home runs he had made as a junior athlete. Harry was able to rethink and re-examine how wonderful and relaxed he felt back then. Later, Harry shared about unhappy childhood experiences. He realized how tense his body would get while he listened to his own heavy breathing. Memories of his parents arguing would flood his mind. However, because Harry allowed himself to recall the good times and stayed with the good feelings, it opened the door for Harry to start using PRT's "Sitting and Listening" technique with less resistance.

Now that Harry was more attentive to his relaxed senses and of his more neutral thoughts, he was able to apply his PRT "Creating

Alternatives" technique. For Harry, this technique came to him when he accepted accountability for his own actions. He started by making a list of goals for himself that would improve his relationship with Sally. Also, now that Harry had regained his ability to talk about his fears since his childhood trauma, he could make a list of all his fears he had about his relationship with Sally, about women in general, and "Execute" his Plan by communicating those fears with Sally.

Teaching Sally how to use PRT's "Sitting and Listening" technique was also a little rough at first, much like it was for Harry. However, by allowing her to set the "stage" in my office, she was able to feel more relaxed which helped her begin to use this technique successfully. Because of her trust issues, she asked if she could keep her eyes open during the "Sitting and Listening" technique. Sally also asked if I would turn around and not see her as she proceeded with this technique. As Sally started paying attention to her own breathing and not allowing any positive and negative thoughts interfere with her "Sitting and Listening" technique, she came to some self discoveries about herself, which she later shared during her "Rethinking and Re-examining" technique.

Sally realized in the "Rethinking and Re-examining" technique how her thoughts and feelings felt disconnected from her body. She remembered how she taught herself to mentally disconnect herself from her body when her uncle sexually abused her. Sally also discovered in her "Rethinking and Re-examining" technique that she was overcompensating for her mother putting a mental "gag" in her mouth not to speak. As a result of this overcompensation, Sally became outspoken as an adult as well as needing to have the "upper hand" in her relationships with men.

By Sally finally removing that mental "gag" from her own mouth, she was able to set off an array of "Creating Alternatives" for herself to choose from in "Executing Her Plan." She had expressed her experience as, "a liberating freedom to speak and to know what I want now and to share my needs with Harry."

When Harry and Sally 's own PRT "Sitting and Listening" techniques were brought together, both Harry and Sally learned how to listen better to each other's PRESENT thoughts and feelings. I would reiterate to Harry and Sally that PRT's "Sitting and Listening" technique is about being attentive in THAT moment to the thoughts and feelings expressed by the other person. I instructed both Harry and Sally to do the following: first, before speaking, take a slow deep breath in and then also exhale slowly. Second, make eye contact with other each as much as possible throughout this technique. Third, each person alternate by one person sharing one clear sentence of what he/she is thinking or feelings at that moment. Four, the person who was listening repeat back to the other person what he/she said.

In Harry and Sally 's own PRT "Rethinking and Re-examining" technique, they both had to come to some "tough love" realizations about themselves that they were now ready to share with one another. Each person relied on telling lies to each other and then rationalized those lies to theoretically prevent them from causing the other any more emotional pain. Encouraging Harry and Sally to reexamine their own spoken statements helped them see how many self-contradicting statements were being spoken between the both of them. They both realized that their own self-contradicting statements created a major mental barrier for building trust in their relationship. Another realization that both Harry and Sally found out through the use of "Rethinking and Re-examining" technique was that they both had unhealed emotional scars from childhood traumas. As a result, any incidents that triggered suppressed thoughts and feelings from that trauma forced the use of mental barriers.

Harry and Sally's own "Creating Alternatives" and "Executing Your Plan" came from each of them understanding that they must take personal accountability of their own actions in order to start improving their relationship with each other. Harry and Sally's relationship improved because now they both had a clear understanding of their own needs. They learned how to follow through with their needs, which boosted self-confidence and lessened the threat to be overpowered by the other person.

Following through with our own needs is not an easy thing to do. Especially when the unexpected happens like your elderly parent getting ill and you immediately become the caregiver for that parent because your other parent is too frail to take care of his/her spouse.

PRT AND THE SANDWICH GENERATION

When the term Sandwich generation came out years ago, it was defined as people needing to care for their aging parents while supporting their minor children. Today, the Sandwich generation has extended its meaning, not only to include minor children, but also adult children who still live at home. As the baby boomer generation is now reaching old age, the phrase, "Sandwich generation" is becoming a common household name as in the case with Doris.

Doris had finally reached a point in her life where she was happily enjoying the "fruits of Her Labor." She had a healthy and harmonious balance with her family, with work and with church activities. Doris was managing all of life's elements successfully, giving her an abundance of quality time in every aspect of her life. In fact, this balance gave Doris a sense of personal pride that others saw her as being a self-sufficient woman. And then the unexpected happened.

Doris was a loving daughter who was attentive to and had regular phone contact with her elderly parents who lived alone in an adult community. One late night, Doris got an urgent call from her worried mother that her father had fallen in the bathroom. Doris' father was diagnosed with Alzheimer's years ago. His disease had advanced very quickly. And because of her mother's health problem with osteoporosis, her mother could no longer physically care for him. Doris could not have imaged the emotional and relationship challenges she would have to face after her parents moved in with her and her family.

Her father's doctors identified Doris, as her father's official "caregiver." Doris was now part of the sandwich generation. For Doris, managing the house responsibilities now forced her to "squeeze" in added responsibilities by taking her father to his doctor visits, administering his medication and fighting daily on the phone with health insurance companies. Doris began feeling very stressed out. And shortly after her many life changes Doris started feeling depressed. She found herself having problems sleeping, losing interest in going to her church and getting easily irritated with her husband and children. Doris even started having health problems of her own.

The first time Doris walked into my office, she had guilt ridden over her face for taking time off from her busy schedule. She felt guilty about coming to therapy to talk about herself instead of attending to the needs of her family. Her thoughts seemed to be bouncing back and forth from trying to pay attention to what I was saying and trying to remember what tasks were left to do before the end of the day. Shortly after the session started, Doris realized she might as well listen since she was paying for the session and was going to be in session for an hour.

It did not take long for Doris to start using Personal Revolution Therapy's "Sitting and Listening" technique in the session. She was now sitting back on the sofa and looking more relaxed. Her tense facial muscles were gone now and she looked like she was feeling a gentle breeze upon her face. As Doris was paying more attention to her own breathing, she started to slowly inhale through her nose and exhale slowly through her mouth as if she had done this before. Doris doing PRTs "Sitting and Listening" technique reminded her of how relaxed she became when she prayed at her church. She would sit still in her chair; close her eyes and breath softly as she prayed.

Doris was able to feel more comfortable with herself as a caregiver by applying the PRT "Rethinking and Re-examining" technique. This technique helped her recognize some stereotypes and stigma associated with a caregiver asking for help. She worried that if she asked for help, she would lose her 'self-sufficient' status in the eyes of societal expectations. By reexamining that caring for her family was more important than worrying about what other people thought, her spirits began to lift. Doris with "rethinking" her role as a caregiver helped her realize that asking for help was not a sign of weakness. Finally, Doris discovered that, as a caregiver, she also needed self-pampering to recharge her mental batteries in order to be sufficient in caring for her family.

Because Doris had been successful in the past in managing her time, adjusting and executing her priorities through the use of PRT "Creating and Prioritizing" technique, came to her somewhat naturally. From her "Alternatives" list Doris started delegating new household responsibilities to her husband and children. She allowed herself to ask extended family members for respite care for her parents. She arranged a carpool with other parents in taking the children to school. Doris also made time for herself and started attending her church services regularly again.

In the case with Doris, she had to learn how to deal with present day stress while learning and using PRT skills. Harry and

Sally both had childhood traumas to contend with while they also learned how to incorporate PRT into their daily lives. Learning a new skill takes time and patience and primarily the willingness to change. Eventually, all three of the people in this story were able to live a more balanced life for themselves and with those they love. But what happens in the case when someone suffers from addiction? Can PRT be effective in changing their lives as well?

PRT and Addiction

When I first met Debbie, she was a very distraught twenty-two year old addict. "I can't get my life straighten out," said Debbie when I first met her. Unfortunately, her addiction started almost ten years earlier. When Debbie was in middle school, her troubles started as she began skipping school and experimenting with alcohol and marijuana. By the time Debbie was in high school, she was smoking marijuana daily and drinking alcohol heavily every weekend. When she reached her senior year of high school, Debbie began having blackouts. At the age of eighteen Debbie would stay out for days without notifying her parents of her whereabouts. To her parent's dismay, Debbie repeatedly either dropped out or refused to attend every substance abuse program that her parents tried enrolling her in. Debbie said the only reason she agreed to come and see me was because her boyfriend's mother was a good friend of mine and because her boyfriend threatened to break up with her if she didn't seek help.

Debbie learned how to use PRT's "Sitting and Listening" technique after she learned first how to use the "Rethinking and Re-examining" technique. It was further into her other sessions that she was finally able to return to learning this first technique. Each time Debbie tried to pay attention to her breathing and calm her thoughts, she became mentally detoured and started crying and venting over how horrible her parents had treated her growing up. For now, I was doing the Listening for her as she let out her feelings. This helped her relieve a lot of the emotional distress she was feeling. Sitting and Listening and being a surrogate to Debbie showed her how the "Sitting and Listening" technique is used. This helped her "plant the seed" for later when she was able to do her own PRT "Sitting and Listening." Once Debbie was willing to take accountability for her own actions she was ready for "Sitting and Listening."

When Debbie used Personal Revolution Therapy "Rethinking and Re-examining" technique she was able to talk about how bad she thought others had treated her. She was also able to look at how her thoughts had affected her throughout her life. Debbie started recalling that as a very young child she would get easily upset when she did not get her way. Because Debbie could not shake off her frustration, her mother would get impatient with her and start belittling her. Sometimes, her mother would physically shake her and say, "What is wrong with you?" Debbie recalled her mother also referring to her as, "an ungrateful child."

As she got a little older Debbie remembered feeling moments of happiness for no reason, but her happy feelings never lasted long. Debbie remembered thinking of how much she had wanted to get that happy feeling back as a kid. She remembered the first time she drank alcohol and how that brought back her pseudo happy feelings. Debbie realized that smoking marijuana and drinking alcohol was the only thing that "calmed me down" back then. Debbie recalled, "Even when I was high on pot and my mother didn't notice, we sometimes had a nice time together."

Debbie started to realize how much she depended on alcohol to make her feel better. She rationalized her drinking by saying such things as; "it gives me some type of normalcy in my life." It took awhile for Debbie to accept the fact that alcohol really was not making her life better as she continued to use PRT "Rethinking and Re-examining" technique. As Debbie began to challenge her own thoughts about what was real and what was not, she started to see the world as less scary. It also helped her accept that people are not all bad or all good, including her mother, who helped improve their relationship.

In session, Debbie was able to "Create and Prioritize her Alternatives, but in "Executing her Plan," that was another story. Debbie realized that she might have a mental illness and agreed to get a psychiatric evaluation for possible medication. She also agreed to start attending Alcoholics Anonymous meetings. Debbie even agreed to bring her mother to counseling to help her improve her relationship with her. Unfortunately, as quickly as she got motivated to start improving her life, she just as quickly got discouraged about putting her plan into action once she left each counseling session.

Debbie's pattern of having mixed emotions became predictable. She would drop out of therapy for a while, relapse on alcohol again, and when things got really bad she would call to make an appointment to come in again for therapy. It was not until much later, when Debbie decided she wanted to strengthen her Jewish faith, that her emotions stabilized enough for her to start the PRT "Executing Your Plan" technique. Many times addiction arises as a result of poor coping skills from not having the opportunity as teenagers to learn good relationships skills.

PRT AND TEENAGERS

When parents use PRT techniques in their relationship with teenagers, it helps the teenager accept accountability for his or her actions and improves the communication between the parent and the teenager. I remember Ben at age sixteen being notorious in self-contradiction, which he was unaware of. One day, out of anger he said to his mother, "I hate you and want you out of my life." When Ben's mom used the PRT "Creating and Prioritizing Alternatives" technique, Ben was able to vent his thoughts in a respectful way. Ben's mother asked him clarifying questions such as, "you want me out of your life?" Typically teenagers can become less verbally aggressive if they are allowed to vent their feelings respectfully. By Ben reacting less negatively toward his mother, he was now able to begin using the PRT "Sitting and Listening" and "Creating and Prioritizing Alternatives" techniques. When Ben used the "Sitting and Listening" technique he was able to reflect about his true feelings toward his mother. He started saying things like, "but mom, you are my life." To help Ben see his own self-contradicting statements his mom said to him, "you hate me and want me out of your life and I am your life, right?" This statement allowed Ben to hear and really feel the things he was saying out loud.

I recall another example where I helped Ben's mom apply PRT techniques at home with Ben. I instructed his mom that next time Ben wanted something from her after a disputed argument, to point out to him his self-contradicting statements. Several days later, Ben began arguing disrespectfully with his mother saying, "I hate you and I want you out of my life." Ben walked away and did not say another word to his mother. Like most teenagers, Ben's niceness came out when he wanted something from his mother. The next day Ben asked his mother to borrow the car. His mom responded by using one of her "Creating and Prioritizing Alternatives" that she had decided to use. Instead of saying yes to Ben while he was in the "being nice phase," she held him accountable for his statement from the "anger phase" the night before. She said, "I would love to let you borrow the car right now but I am out of your life." This PRT "Creating and Prioritizing Alternatives" and "Executing Your Plan" helped mom set boundaries with Ben so that he would be more respectful toward her. This in return helped Ben to reevaluate his tactics in communicating with his mother.

Ben began to recognize his self-contradicting statements when his mom started using the PRT techniques. Ben began to understand that his aggressive behavior no longer had a "pull" in manipulating his mother. This led Ben to begin using PRT "Rethinking and Re-examining" technique himself in order to be more aware of his self-contradictory thinking. He was able to reexamine his own thinking about what he really wanted from his mother. This thinking pattern helped Ben explore healthier ways to get what he wanted, which in turn improved his relationship with his mother.

PRT and The Troubled Adolescent

Even troubled adolescents can surprise you when you teach them how to use PRT Techniques. When I met Travis years ago he was only fourteen years old and already he had multiple criminal charges against him of burglary and assault by the juvenile court system. Part of Travis's probation agreement was for him to complete community service hours and to seek therapeutic help.

At first, my goal in helping Travis was to teach him how to use the PRT "Sitting and Listening" technique. I found a location for Travis to do his community service work as well as begin working on "Sitting and Listening." I wanted to take him to a new place that he was both unfamiliar with as well as a place where he would not feel threatened by the people around him. I decided a nursing home would be the perfect place for Travis to fulfill both tasks.

When Travis entered the nursing home for the first time, I encouraged him to pay attention to his breathing while at the same time trying to remember as many details of the building and of the people as possible. By Travis paying attention to his breathing and seeing the unfortunate conditions of not only the building but also of the sick and frail elderly, it helped him stay calm and attentive to his surroundings. He soon gained a sense of curiosity of how warm he was being greeted there by the elderly and the staff.

Then I helped Travis use the PRT " Rethinking and Re-examining" technique, which allowed him to clarify and organize some to his emotional experiences he had at the nursing home. At first he described his experience at the nursing home as being "weird." Allowing Travis to talk more about his experiences at the nursing home helped him see positive things about himself that he was unaware of before. His "weird" experience of meeting the elderly at the nursing home turned around when he noticed they seemed to genuinely want to meet him without prejudice. This was a new experience for Travis. The experience of unconditional acceptance helped Travis bring out his compassionate side. His use of the "Reexamining" technique allowed him to explore his own needs. He first wanted to know why many of those elderly at the nursing home lived in such poor conditions. Then, he began thinking of ways to help them. Travis would later discover by gaining self-confidence in helping the elderly allowed him to gain self-confidence in helping himself by wanting better things in his life.

Travis was able to use the PRT "Creating and Prioritizing Alternatives" technique to find ways of helping the elderly each time he visited the nursing home. This in turn helped him improve his social skills. Because Travis felt emotionally safe and comfortable there, he was able to be available not only to help the elderly at the nursing home but also to improve his willingness to be more social. His mission to help the elderly was clear now.

By Travis using the PRT "Executing Your Plan" technique, it helped him engage more in positive conversations with the elderly and he was more willing to help them with simple tasks.

As expected, Travis started bonding with many of the elderly at the nursing home. I recall Ruby, one of the people in the nursing home that Travis bonded with, was a small statured woman who suffered with severe arthritis. One day while Ruby was sitting in her wheelchair her sweater fell to the floor. Without hesitation, Travis reached down to pick up Ruby's sweater and he placed it back on her wheelchair. Ruby said thank you to him and he politely responded with, "you are welcome." By Travis repeatedly "Executing" his Plan" to help the elderly at the nursing home he no longer felt "weird." As a matter of fact, such repeated positive acts of compassion for others helped him feel better about himself. His new PRT techniques helped improve his self-esteem and self-confidence. This new sense of self helped Travis apply PRT to other areas of his life, which helped him build a brighter future for himself.

PRT Techniques to reach peak performance in Sports

Throughout my years of clinical practice, I have helped amateur and professional athletes improve their game by using PRT techniques. For these athletes, their "Executing Plan" is to display peak performance in each game they play. Many professional athletes know that in order to have peak performance during their game, they must mentally establish being "in the zone." When you are "in the zone," you are playing your best and not allowing any distractions from interference during your peak performance. PRT techniques help athletes improve their mental game by helping them be "in the Zone" and maintain a clear and calm mind. Athletes who use PRT techniques are able to stay focused and quickly readjust to distractions that may interfere with their peak performance. Many athletes I have worked with have shared that they were also able to use PRT techniques to improve personal relationships. These athletes who experience being "in the zone," are experiencing total concentration on their peak performance. Having proper PRT techniques at their disposal prevents distractions and allows athletes to continually achieve peak performance.

PRT techniques are easily transferable to all issues in all of your relationships that are indirectly preventing you from reaching your own peak performance. At play, "Executing your Plan" gives you that "In the zone" peak performance experience. Maintaining clear thoughts and clear alternatives with a high level of self-confidence fuels peak performance.

I remember Don, a middle age golf instructor in West Palm Beach. Don wanted to work on qualifying for the Senior PGA Tour. I recall listening to other golfers speak of Don's impeccable golf swing. However, what Don lacked was consistency in his game, which is what separates an amateur golfer from a professional golfer. Don's inconsistency to play golf well each time he got on the golf course is no different than the inconsistencies of being in an unfulfilled relationship. Every time Don played golf he never knew if the next time he played would bring him any level of satisfaction. Just like in an unhappy relationship. Will the next encounter with that person bring any level of satisfaction for you?

I began to teach Don PRT techniques the same way I often do with others accept, I was doing the training with him on the golf course. In Don's case, the focus of PRT's "Sitting and Listening" technique was to help Don slow down his unproductive thinking through PRT's breathing exercises. In relationships, as well as in sports, Don's chronic non-productive thinking was being fed by memories of unsuccessful trial and tribulations of missed opportunities. Don's lack of confidence in his game brought feelings of regret and self-doubt.

Once Don was able to reduce his rapid negative thinking through the use of PRT "Sitting and Listening" technique, he was able to stay mentally in the present. Don's next challenge was changing his negative mental attitude toward his golf game. He then began using technique #2, "Rethinking and Re-examining," in order to understand where his "mental" game was suffering. Through a series of questions regarding his beliefs of how his negative thoughts came to be in the first place, was the start to re-examining his thought process. This helped Don transform his mental golf game of self-negativity by establishing the "Rethinking and Re-examining" technique for a successful "playbook" rather than one filled with self-doubt. Both "Sitting and Listening" as well as "Rethinking and Re-examining" helped him develop a mental toolbox for him to use when playing golf. "Rethinking and Re-examining" help us discover the root of where our present thoughts and feelings come from.

As Don started to understand the mental roots of his negative thinking about his golf game, he discovered revolutionary truths about WHY he thought the way he thought. Don was able to understand that his negativity and self-doubt about his golf game came from his critical and unsupported father who never approved of Don making a living playing golf. Our parents are our greatest influence in how we are going to relate to others and how we are going to handle difficult circumstances in the future. Don repeatedly thought of his father's negativity toward him as the one distraction that kept him from reaching a level of peak performance.

One of Don's challenges was helping him write out his "Creating Alternatives." In all of us, shifting our negative attitudes toward healthier ones can be challenging at first. But once you pass through that threshold, there is no going back! Once Don had a list of healthier mental attitudes, he was able to "let go" of hoarding negative attitudes about his game. He was ready to write out his more positive mental "playbook." Some of Don's "Creating Alternatives" in his playbook was to be attentive to his breathing when playing. The breathing helped him stay focused and prevented any negative thinking from resurfacing. This helped Don become more confidence in his technical golf game without self-doubts. This for Don made "Executing his Plan" effortless in improving his game.

PRT AND HEALTH CARE

PRT techniques help patients communicate more effectively with their doctors. Because of improved communication, the relationship and trust between patient and doctor is greatly improved. Let us look at how one patient improved her health as a result of using the PRT techniques.

Monica was a middle-aged woman who was referred to me by her primary healthcare physician because her doctor thought she was depressed. Monica had been suffering with chronic pain since a car accident several years before. Monica admitted she was feeling depressed because she felt the medication she was taking was not helping relieve her chronic pain. Monica was also feeling discouraged with her doctor because she had followed up with all of her doctor's recommendation, but still there was no relief of her chronic pain. After months of traveling, seeing different medical specialists one after another and attending various physical therapy treatments, Monica said she found minimal relief for her pain. The process of discovering a solution to her pain also left Monica feeling exhausted and overwhelmed. Monica began feeling hopeless and helpless and as a result she grew depressed.

As I introduced Monica to the Personal Revolution Therapy "Sitting and Listening" technique, I included some visual guided imagery to help her stay focused. Soon after Monica started paying attention to her breathing, I instructed her to visualize a soothing blue light on top of her head. I helped Monica guide that image to travel inside her body starting from her head to her toes, touching gently all the muscles in her body. Each time Monica was able to visualize the soothing blue light traveling down her body, she would take a deep breath. By the time she guided the soothing blue light to her toes, her breathing had slowed down. Monica shared that she began to feel more relaxed and that her chronic pain had actually started to subside some. For Monica, using the "Sitting and Listening" technique became a daily technique that helped her relax more which reduced some of her chronic pain.

When Monica began using PRT "Rethinking and Re-examining" technique, she started realizing she needed to become more assertive with her doctors by asking more questions about her medical condition. Asking questions empowered Monica to be part of the decision making about her health. Her Rethinking process led her to see that by nature she was a meek person and that she had grown up as a child believing you don't question authority figures. Also, the Reexamining technique helped her see she has always wanted to be liked by everyone. She did not want to upset people she would come in contact with, especially doctors who supposedly knew what to do regarding her health. When Monica used the PRT "Rethinking and Re-examining" technique, she concluded how silly it was for a middle aged woman to worry if people would like her or not. Releasing that mental burden of what others thought of her, prepared her to move on to the next PRT technique, "Creating and Prioritizing Alternatives."

At first, Monica was very cautious in using the PRT "Creating and Prioritizing Alternatives" technique for fear that by "Executing Her Plan" she would offend her doctors, but later she became less worried and more focused on finding solutions to relieve her chronic pain. One of Monica's Alternatives was to start using the Internet to learn as much as possible about chronic pain. Based on the information she gathered about chronic pain, she compiled a list of questions to ask her doctors. Another of her Prioritizing Alternative's was to make a mental note for herself to stop the doctor each time she did not understand the doctor's explanation and ask for clarification. As Monica became more assertive with her doctors, her doctor's became more encouraged to communicate more frequently with Monica about her medical progress. This in turn helped Monica make the best possible medical decision in order to relieve her chronic pain.

PRT and Dieting

"No matter what type of diet I am on, I just can't seem to lose weight," said Megan, a woman in her mid-forties. "I might as well accept the fact that I will never lose weight again and be miserable for the rest of my life," she added. At home, each time Megan started a new diet plan; her boyfriend and her children would raise their "caution flags" to one another to watch out for Megan's moodiness. Ignoring her doctor's suggestions to avoid certain unhealthy diet programs, her doctor noticed a change in her hormones that were thought to be contributing to her feeling depressed.

As far back as Megan could remember, food was always an important topic in family conversations. "Eat all the food on your plate so you can grow up to be a beautiful girl," her parents frequently commented. During her pre-adolescent years, Megan began noticing how much popular culture rewarded thinness. If she was thin and could wear the latest fashions, Megan noticed her girlfriends would not ridicule her. As a popular cheerleader in high school, Megan remembered becoming more preoccupied with food. If she felt that she was gaining weight, she would starve herself for several days until she reached her desired weight. This led to many arguments between her and her parents over her poor eating habits. It was not until after Megan got married that she focused less on her weight. She wanted to pay more attention to starting a family and raising her children.

It was after her divorce that Megan vigorously embarked again in wanting to lose weight. Unfortunately, her marriage ended in divorce when her children were still in elementary school. Megan continued to focus on raising her children as a single mother. It was not until all of her children had reached high school and her supportive, yet badgering girlfriends begged her to "go out and meet a nice guy." Megan started wanting to lose weight once again. At first, she felt confident that she would lose weight as easily as she did when she was a teenager. However, she unfortunately discovered that her metabolism was processing at a much slower rate now that she was older. Megan's effort to lose weight became more difficult than she thought it would.

Megan was unable to lose weight after trying several diet programs and became chronically frustrated. She started having problems with sleeping because she was unable to relax. When Megan started using the PRT "Sitting and Listening" technique, her attentiveness to her own slow breathing helped her reduce tension in her body. At first, Megan would forcefully inhale and exhale with her mouth only, which made it difficult for her to relax her body and made it easy for her to lose her concentration. Her urgency to quickly learn this technique mirrored her frustration over not being able lose weight easily. As I continued to instruct her on how to use this PRT technique, Megan began noticing how relaxed her body was becoming. However, each time Megan lost concentration on her breathing, her body tensed up again. I encouraged Megan to practice this technique more times at home so she would gain more self-confidence in her ability to use this technique. This helped her slow down her thoughts and to relax more.

As Megan began using the PRT "Rethinking and Re-examining" technique, she been to realize it was not necessarily those diet programs that prevented her from losing weight, rather it was her negative outlook on food that was preventing her from losing weight. As Megan started reexamining her thoughts, she started to reflect on her childhood memories. These memories led her to take note that each time her family gathered together to socialize, it revolved around food. "Eat something dear, you look too skinny," her relatives constantly told her. To please her relatives, she would eat something even though she was not hungry. During her adolescent years, Megan began believing that food was an obstacle to losing weight. Megan started feeling resentful and untrustworthy toward any family member that would give her advice about the right way to eat. Because Megan wanted to avoid any family member from "nagging" her about food, she just ate whether she was hungry or not. For Megan, eating became a way to suppress those resentful and untrustworthy feelings she had toward her family. Eating also became an unpleasant reminder of her elder relatives telling her what is good or bad for her to eat.

Since diet programs require a person to closely follow its rules, Megan found most diets programs became just another authoritative family member. Quitting diet programs was Megan's unconscious way to rebel. Megan realized she needed to be more accountable in taking steps toward having a positive experience while in a diet program if she really wanted to lose weight.

Megan realized if she was to succeed in losing weight, she needed to change BOTH her eating habits and her attitude about food. In using the PRT "Creating and Prioritizing Alternatives" technique, Megan started exploring ways of how to feel more positive about food. First, she needed to make an appointment with her doctor to determine the best type of diet program for her to enroll in based on her biological makeup. Then, she needed to search for a diet program that fit her own metabolic type. Finally, she needed to find ways to "let go" of her resentful feelings from her past. She decided to write letters to each family member and share her feelings as a way to vent.

When Megan used the PRT "Executing your Plan" technique she created a healthier lifestyle for herself by finally losing the weight and keeping the weight off. By knowing her own metabolic makeup, she was able to communicate more effectively with her diet program advisor. When she saw she was not gaining weight after eating the right foods, her attitude about food changed. Also, Megan resolved her resentful feelings toward her family by just writing her frustrations out in letterform to her family. Her venting through writing was enough. Megan decided she did not need to mail the letters to find closure.

PRT AND PLASTIC SURGERY

As a consultant for patients at a plastic surgeon's office, I have helped patients learn how to use PRT Techniques to achieve a positive outcome after their plastic surgery. I discovered that many patients who decide to have elective cosmetic surgery have unrealistic expectations. Many patients believe that plastic surgery is going to improve personal conflicted relationships. In Arlene's case, during her initial consultation with her doctor for elective plastic surgery, she had expressed having a history of emotional problems since her childhood years. She believed that by having plastic surgery she would feel better about herself. Before her doctor agreed to proceed with the surgery I was called in for a consultation.

Arlene was in her late thirties and found herself less attractive. As she aged, she felt anxious that aging was not helping her look any better. Her gynecologist informed her that her body had started the perimenopausal stage. Arlene noticed her sexual intimacy with her partner had changed. She discovered it took her longer to get sexually aroused and that her organisms did not last as long as before. She believed this was a reason why she was having relationship problems with her partner. Her bodily changes made her feel that her life was unmanageable.

Arlene began to feel more anxious as time went on and it became difficult for her to relax. In helping Arlene to be better prepared for her upcoming plastic surgery, I showed her how to use PRT techniques.

The PRT "Sitting and Listening" technique helped Arlene slow down her rapid thoughts and to relax more easily. As Arlene started to use the PRT "Sitting and Listening" technique, her inhaling and exhaling became smoother and less pressured. Arlene struggled at first in staying focused on her breathing, but over time she began feeling more relaxed which allowed deeper thoughts about her childhood experiences to arise. I reassured Arlene this was normal especially for those who had tough childhoods. By hearing the reassurance that her thoughts were normal, Arlene was able to trust and use the PRT 'Sitting and Listening" technique.

Arlene realized by using the PRT 'Rethinking and Re-examining" technique that it helped her have a better perspective over her life. This perspective helped her understand why her childhood issues had resurfaced. Because Arlene was able to have more realistic expectations about those emotional issues, she was able to later enjoy the outcome of her elective plastic surgery.

As Arlene continued to use the PRT "Rethinking and Re-examining" techniques, it reminded her of when she went to counseling years ago. She thought that she had worked through her childhood traumas the first time she was in counseling. She recalled growing up as a child feeling powerless to do anything that helped resolve the fighting in her family. Back when she was in counseling, Arlene learned to identify and focus more on issues she was capable of being in control of and less focused on issues that were out of her control. As Arlene began reexamining her thoughts as to why these childhood memories returned, she realized when she finished counseling she was young and vibrant. Those feelings of attractiveness helped motivate Arlene toward fulfilling her dreams at the same time feeling as though she had resolved many of her childhood traumas. At that time she also became financially independent and was able to have and maintain healthy relationships. Regarding her relationship with her dysfunctional family, she was able to set boundaries with them so that it would not interfere with her well-being. Arlene felt she had control of her emotional state by taking responsibility for things in her life.

In remembrance of her personal achievements when she was in therapy, Arlene started to believe in herself again. She was then able to proceed in using the PRT "Creating and Prioritizing Alternatives" and 'Executing your Plan" techniques. Arlene began to remember the written goals she had set for herself back when she was in counseling. She used some of those written goals to create her "Alternatives." She focused on building alternatives that she knew she could execute. She no longer simply wanted to improve her physical appearance, but she also wanted to change her lifestyle from eating better to communicating better with her partner. These alternatives became the ingredients in helping Arlene feel more emotionally stable. She realized that elective plastic surgery was not a "short cut" in resolving life stressors or relationship problems. Since Arlene no longer had any hidden agendas as to why she wanted plastic surgery, she was able to enjoy the outcome as something she wanted to do for her and for her alone.

As a note, I noticed that many patients who seek elective cosmetic plastic surgery often decide to proceed for the wrong reasons such as emotional stability, improved self-esteem, and rewarding interpersonal relationships. All these can be accomplished by using PRT techniques, but not by having elective cosmetic plastic surgery.

PRT AND THE WORKPLACE

The first time I met Bob in my office, he was not happy to be there. His employer "strongly" advised him to see a counselor because of his poor attitude at work. Because he was in upper management, his negativism was affecting the morale of other employees. Bob believed he did not have any problems with other employees. Instead he felt, "people there have problems with me." He had accepted the fact that the reason why other employees did not like him was because he was in management. For Bob, all managers are disliked because managers have to tell their employees what to do. He added, " People do not like to be told what to do." It was only after his boss witnessed an argument between Bob and another employer that his boss insisted he get help.

Many of Bob's responses regarding his family were often described as indifference. He expressed no major family conflicts with his wife or children. He described his family home life as "normal like any other family." He provided little information about the relationships he has between himself, his wife and his children. One of the few comments he did share was that his father had died from cancer several months before therapy. He did not disclose much about his past relationship with his father except that his father was mean when he was growing up and that his father had a short temper. Bob also shared his contact with siblings was minimal, usually only once a month by phone and most of those phone conversations with them were brief and superficial. The only time they got together was during the holidays.

When I presented Bob with how to use the PRT "Sitting and Listening" technique he was reluctant at first, but later found this technique helpful especially as a deterrent from starting any nasty arguments with employees at work. At first, Bob half-heartedly attempted to use this technique, but worried that if he refused to participate in therapy that I would report back to his boss that he was noncompliant with counseling. Bob was using his Employee Assistance Program (EAP) through his job to pay for his counseling sessions. The EAP required that I report my clinical findings and recommendations of Bob to his boss.

After I reassured Bob that I would discuss my clinical results first with him before contacting anyone, Bob seemed less guarded and more willing to start learning how to use the PRT "Sitting and Listening" technique. In the beginning, Bob's body language was fidgety and his breathing was tense. As he improved his focus on his breathing he began to slow down. He began to notice how quiet the therapy room was the more he was able to focus on his surroundings, which helped him relax even more. To Bob's surprise he had not realized how "listening" to silence helped him calm his thoughts. He would later discover that by using the PRT "Sitting and Listening" technique daily at work, that it kept him from reacting negatively toward his co-workers.

It was rough for Bob at first to use the Personal Revolution Therapy "Rethinking and Re-examining" technique, but as he got more comfortable in talking about his frustrations without "blowing up," he was able to re-examine his own thoughts and get a better perspective about his misdirected anger. In the beginning when Bob was learning how to use this technique, he hesitated to talk about himself. He rarely allowed himself to reflect and talk about on his own feelings. To TALK OUT his frustrations were something that was foreign for him. Instead he was more accustomed to verbally attack others who frustrated him.

After several sessions Bob became more comfortable talking about himself. As he began "Re-examining" his thoughts, Bob realized that having unpleasant thoughts did not have to lead him to react negatively to those thoughts. Once Bob was able to separate his thoughts from his actions, he was able to accept his feelings and stop the way he had treated his co-workers in the past. He also began to re-examine the causes of his suppressed anger toward members of his extended family, especially his father.

It took awhile for Bob to learn how to use the "Creating and Prioritizing Alternatives" technique as well as the "Execute your Plan" technique. He needed more time and experience in using these PRT techniques for him to feel more comfortable in using them daily without falling back to his old ways. But as Bob shared more successful stories of when he did apply the PRT techniques, despite some early setbacks, his self-confidence in using the techniques improved. As a boy Bob was never taught how to have effective coping skills to work through his own feelings. As a result, this made it difficult in creating healthy alternatives to improve his relationship with his co-workers. One of Bob's "Prioritizing Alternatives" was to learn how to communicate effectively with his co-workers and in other personal relationships.

Bob used the PRT "Executing your Plan" technique to help control his temper. Each time he started feeling frustrated with his co-workers, Bob reverted back to using the PRT "Sitting and Listening" technique to help him calm his thoughts. His boss noticed Bob excusing himself from the room when he would start getting frustrated with his co-workers. This gave Bob time to compose his thoughts away from others. When he returned to the room, Bob used his newly learned communication skills with his co-workers to better express himself. He was also able to listen better to the needs of his co-workers. This healthier exchange of workers relating with one another helped improve the productivity of the company. Bob eventually ended up using PRT techniques in his personal life as well.

··PART IV··

Insightful Information:
Why We Stay The Same

Fearing The Unknown

Unfortunately, I have seen and heard within my clinical practice and in the community at large, that many people complain of feeling unsatisfied and unhappy in their relationships! Why do so many people stay in an unhappy relationship for years? Without having the skills to tackle problems effectively in any type of problematic relationship, we fear that that relationship will bring more suffering if we try to make any attempt to solve those problems. For one reason, persons in unskilled relationships fear those problems may affect their financial stability. Therefore, those who have been in unhappy relationships for a long time stay together for OTHER reasons THAN working on improving their relationship directly.

In long unhappy relationships, if we do not know how to regain that emotional safe connection with the other person, we look and focus on what the other person in that unhappy relationship can give us, such as material things or sex. In some cases, sometimes we get more anxious if we were to apply any new or better coping skills in solving our relationship problems. Sometimes we think that if we "rock the boat" in trying to fix that relationship that we will create more problems to that existing bad relationship. If that happens, we would put ourselves in a more vulnerable position that could threaten the already weak stability of that relationship. I hear people say things like, "Let's just leave things as they are. At least we are surviving day to day." The advantage of using PRT techniques is that it removes the fears that prevent us from moving forward.

NEGATIVE THINKING LEADS TO
NEGATIVE EXPERIENCES

Without effective coping skills such as the Personal Revolution Therapy techniques that allow you to work through difficult relationships, we usually end up having negative feelings toward that other person. PRT techniques prevent the communication in a conflicted relationship to turn into an exchange of nagging comments between two people. Without applying PRT techniques, we have chronic feelings of powerlessness, become overly anxious, or even indifferent about that relationship such as in the case with Bob. We get mentally stuck and surrender to the negative circumstances that exist in that bad relationship. Our negative thinking starts by us justifying our inability to do anything positive about improving that relationship. We even complain to other people about how bad our relationship is or we surrender by saying something like "well, it could be worse. Have you seen how the market is now? I can't afford to do anything about this relationship now. He/she is not that bad. Plus, I kinda got used to the way he/she does things around here anyway."

PRT techniques help us resolve negative thinking in our unresolved relationships. That negative thinking tends to carry over to destructive behaviors against yourself or the other person with whom you are having problems. When we are frustrated in not being able to find ways to resolve relationship problems, we sometimes take our frustration out on others. For example, if we do not use the PRT "Creating and Prioritizing Alternatives" technique for options to help us solve our marital discord, then we might have the tendency to act impulsively without looking closely at the repercussions. Using PRT "Rethinking and Re-examining" technique helps explore those repercussions. Any unresolved negative thinking over a conflicted romantic relationship increases our chances to commit infidelity, for example. For adolescents who have no coping skills and feel there is no escape from "annoying" parents are at a greater risk in experimenting with illicit drugs.

USING UNPRODUCTIVE MENTAL TACTICS

Without PRT techniques to help us resolve problems in our relationships, we let our distressed emotions take control over our decision-making. Without PRT techniques, we are always guided by our distressed emotions, not by working out our problems. We are more likely to make mistakes in our difficult relationship because we are driven only by our distressed emotions. Decision-making that comes from not knowing how to use PRT techniques to deal with our distressed emotions lead us to react more impulsively to find a quick fix or a "Band-Aid." In our distressed state of mind we want to relieve our emotional suffering immediately without allowing ourselves to explore the causes of the problem. Without PRT techniques we start using **mental tactics** as a means to relieve emotional suffering. I define **mental tactics** to be our desperate ways of trying to fix a difficult relationship without having a clear understanding of what we want out of that relationship and not having a clear plan of handling that relationship without attacking the integrity of anyone, including yourself. Mental tactics are how we survive unmanageable relationships. Mental tactics try and convince us we are able to handle the most stressful situations when in reality we are not. We grow to become unhealthy individuals when all we have are mental tactics. How do I know if I am using any mental tactics?

When our breathing is not calm and our body tenses up with the urgency to do ANYTHING at that moment in desperation to get emotional relief caused by that difficult relationship, you are using mental tactics. Under the "umbrella" of unproductive mental tactics, we are forced to believe that our world could come to an end if we do not stop our suffering NOW. We believe that since the other person has control over our feelings, thoughts and actions, that we must somehow manipulate that relationship in order for our distressed emotions to go away. Without personal accountability of our emotions, thoughts or actions, we will never have inner peace. We use unproductive mental tactics with others to run away from our suffering. How do I recognize if someone is using unproductive mental tactics on me?

Without PRT techniques, unhealthy relationships rely on lies as tools to manipulate the other person in that relationship. If the manipulated person in that unhealthy relationship is constantly being told things you want to hear, that is a warning sign that the other person is using unproductive mental tactics on you. Being manipulated is difficult to catch. Another warning sign to watch out for is when that person asks you a construed question to put you on the defense. Examples of both warning signs are statements or questions like, "Why, don't you trust me? You can count on me. You know that I love you. I promise I will change. I'm good for it." Therefore, mental tactics work as MANIPULATORS, manipulating the relationship, instead of effectively working through in resolving the problems of that relationship. What are some mental tactics that we use when we do not yet have PRT techniques to successfully help us improve relationships?

There are many specific mental tactics that people use in place of unlearned coping skills. I chose three manipulating mental tactics that I often see used, not only in my clients, but used by people in general as well. The three most common manipulating mental tactics used are Aggressive, Submissive, and Overcompensating. I will discuss each one in detail.

Aggressive Tactics

Aggressive Tactics are used when we try to manipulate a difficult relationship through invading the rights of the other person to relieve or avoid our own personal suffering. Sometimes these barriers work consciously or unconsciously for some people. The most severe situations of invading the rights of others occur in homes where there is domestic violence. Using financial pressures or even sex to manipulate the other person is another form of Aggressive Tactics. What makes Aggressive Tactics dangerous is that children many times are used as leverages by either parent to manipulate the other.

In many conflicted relationships where coping skills do not exist, verbal threats become the vehicle in Aggressive Tactics against the other person. The goal here is to manipulate the other person to do what you want them to do regardless of how the other person feels. This also occurs in adolescent relationships. As adolescents, learning how to succeed in dating and maintain a healthy and respectful relationship is tough enough. Many adolescents are already driven by their emotions, but having parents there to guide and teach them coping skills reduces the probability for them to be verbally abusive with others. I notice the teenagers who do not have coping skills are more prone to either be verbally abusive to another teenager or they allow themselves to be verbally abused by others. I would hear adolescent girls say things like, "I had to sleep with him or he said that he would dump me." Or they say things like, "I did drugs with him so he wouldn't get mad at me." My main clinical work with teenagers has been helping them apply PRT Techniques to help them cope with peer pressure.

Submissive Tactics

Submissive Tactics are when we try to find ways to escape our own suffering by running away from the other person within that difficult relationship. When we have no PRT techniques in solving our relationship problems we try anything we can to make our suffering stop. Individuals who use Submissive Tactics focus more on finding other means to reduce the overwhelming feelings that arise in being in that difficult relationship, not so much on WHAT that other person has done to you. These overwhelming feelings occur when we do not have PRT techniques to use in dealing with relationship problems. Abusing alcohol or using illicit drugs are the most common use in Submissive Tactics.

Submissive Tactics also are evident in those who focus more on the affairs of other people, including strangers, to escape the anxiety that comes with their inability to resolve difficult relationships that exist in their own lives. Submissive Tactics are present, for example, when any form of entertainment that you use for relaxation and fun turns into an obsession. I define obsession to mean being overly consumed over the lives of others, real or characters, on television. When using Submissive Tactics, we try to mentally block the painful experiences that exist in our difficult relationships. Gossiping is another example of Submissive Tactics. Constantly talking about what someone else is going through in their lives, distracts us from feeling hopelessly depressed or anxious over our own difficult lives.

Overcompensation Tactics

Overcompensation tactics are when we excessively "go overboard" to compensate for our inability to deal with relationship problems effectively. Overcompensation tactics come from the unsolved problems of past personal experiences where you have suffered. You are now eagerly making efforts to assure yourself that those unpleasant experiences do not happen to you again or to anyone else in your family.

For example, lets take the relationship between an overcompensated parent and his/her child. Our own childhood experiences determine how we will raise our children in the future. If very strict parents raised us, which you later in life felt, was poor parenting, as adults the overcompensated parent will tend to go to the extreme and be overly lenient with their own children. In these cases, the defect of the overcompensated parent is that parent not knowing how to balance discipline and nurturing with their children. The overcompensated parent excessively compensates by including the children in ALL family decisions. These parents may also allow their children to do things that may not be age appropriate. Overcompensated parents fail to see that children do need some discipline in order for them to develop self-control.

How about the overcompensated parent who felt that his/her parents were too lenient on him/her? The lenient overcompensated parent may have felt that if his/her own parents had been stricter in their parenting skills with them, the lenient parent would have been more driven for success. As adults, these overcompensated parents become overly disciplinary with his/her own children, leaving no room for that child to develop his/her own individuality. This many times is where parent/child conflict begins.

PRT techniques will prevent you from using unproductive

mental tactics, which interferes with our desire to reach our goals and to create better relationships.

Why We Use Unproductive Mental Tactics

Depending on the type of life experiences, those experiences determine whether we see things clearly or distortedly. **Distorted thinking** brings all sorts of uncertainty in our lives. With distorted thinking, we do not feel safe in our relationships or secure at the workplace. When this happens we shift to survival mode. Survival mode is always an impulsive act for what we think is best for self-preservation, which is actually just an aversion. We sometimes get caught up with the worry of having a nervous breakdown, we do not see what is really going on in our lives and we become blind-sided in seeing reality. Under these conditions, the mind is structured to combat stress in our lives to bring only quick relief. Unfortunately, all the choices that are given are not always the best ones for us. When the sensation of stress becomes overwhelming the mind does anything possible to reduce that stress, even if it means doing things that are not necessarily healthy for you.

Without Personal Revolution Therapy techniques, we develop Mental Tactics to "salvage the wreckage" of a broken heart. Our inability to resolve issues in relationships produces three self-deficiencies that allow the Unproductive Mental Tactics to continue to operate. Without awareness of our behaviors we **Repeat** our own mistakes, we continue to **Lack** self-confidence and we remain **Fearful** of the unknown.

Many times we do not know that we are repeating the same mistakes in trying to fix our relationship. Without PRT coping skills, we may justify lying, for example, as a means to manipulate the relationship. We lie to the other person in our difficult relationship to support our distorted belief that "the truth hurts."

We may say something like, "I don't want to hurt their feelings." Or, "They would be devastated if he/she knew the truth." We also get defensive when we cheat on the other person and then say, "Why, don't you trust me?" We believe things like, "what the other person doesn't know won't hurt them." Repeating the same mistakes in our relationships happens because we continue to find excuses for ourselves, that our actions be justified without allowing ourselves to see the harm that we are causing to ourselves and to others.

The acceptance of unhealthy behaviors continues because neither person in that relationship knows what they want nor do they know how to get it. Stuck in an unsatisfied relationship reinforces our own belief that we lack self-confidence in gaining the things we want in life. The belief we lack confidence to affect change is usually followed by fear. These are some of the roadblocks that keep us from having healthy and meaningful relationships with others and ourselves. This is why the PRT "Rethinking and Re-examining" technique is a crucial step to use in recovering from painful past behaviors. PRT "Rethinking and Re-examining" helps you identify your real personal needs and paves the way in showing you how to get them.

Creating a Better Life With Personal Revolution Therapy (PRT)

The desire to change is difficult no matter what the circumstances are. I found that when clients used the PRT Techniques, they were able to break the "vicious cycle" of constantly feeling disappointed with themselves over failed attempts to improve their lives. PRT techniques are the tools you need to work through your issues. Step by step you will begin to see and feel your success in relationships rather than just distress.

In discovering your own answers through the use of PRT techniques, you are more aware of knowing what you really want, and how you want to execute your plan in improving your relationships and achieving your personal goals. Knowing how to use PRT techniques gives you the mental capacity, gives you self-confidence and motivates you to finally make the changes you desire in improving your own life. Because PRT Techniques help to improve your self-confidence, you will not let others easily sway you from pursuing, improving, and creating a meaningful life for yourself. PRT techniques have changed the lives of many of my clients. PRT has the ability to change your life for the better as well. As you begin to practice PRT in daily life you will truly become Awake and Alive as you experience your personal dreams coming true.

www.ingramcontent.com/pod-product-compliance
Lightning Source LLC
Chambersburg PA
CBHW030411290526
45785CB00004B/1969